I
Eric
America

Poems

Also by Diane Raptosh

Hand Signs from Eternity's Yurt (Kelsay Books, 2022)

Run: A Verse History Victoria Woodhull, published in *Trio* (Etruscan Press Trilogies, 2021)

Dear Z: The Zygote Epistles (Etruscan Press, 2020)

Human Directional (Etruscan Press, 2016)

American Amnesiac (Etruscan Press, 2013)

Parents from a Different Alphabet (Guernica Editions, 2008)

Labor Songs (Guernica Editions, 1999)

Just West of Now (Guernica Editions, 1992)

Diane Raptosh offers us her cultural confessional, taking the topical of our times and personal loss and grief and putting it all through her poetic viewfinder. She delivers brilliant, lyrical, challenging sonnets written with precision and acute imagination. There is a wise oracle speaking in *I Eric America*. The reader is soothed and flattened, absorbed and seen, roiled and substantiated, excavated and understood. Knee-deep in the mishaps of this country she says, "I have no one to world this to but poetry," and we are grateful for her unflinching listings of it all and her hope to find ways "to deputize mercy" in spite of it.

—Diane Jarvenpa, *Shy Lands*

Few American poets these days evade being packaged, labeled, and hawked off by Late Empire's simulacra of culture. And if the Homefront Overlord of these environs is the Techno-Feudalist granite reality we bang our heads on—continuously, then Diane Raptosh's poetics is *the slink of slinks* around those Wall Aesthetics. *I Eric America* is an astonishingly innovative book that brilliantly detects the sparks between pre-social stirrings and post-social debris. The sonnets (44!) are not just malabsorptive to Wall, Gadget, and Master Algorithms, but they passionately express Raptosh's profound kinship with hominids, animals, and plants. *I Eric America* stands as a testament that a maxed-out experimentalism can indeed transform *agape* to endure the most challenging junctures of epochal change.

—Rodrigo Toscano, *The Cut Point*

Diane Raptosh's version of the sonnet explodes the traditional notion of the form as "containing:" Raptosh's 14-line (or in the case of her "sixteenets," 16-line) strophes propel. These are high velocity poems—doe-footed and leaping—they flirt with form while glissading on sound. *I Eric America* is a tour de force of legerdemain with language, not least of which is the title where the poet has made a verb of her brother's name. In 2018, Eric Raptosh was the sole survivor of an aircraft crash that left him with life-altering injuries. The fortitude and creativity with which Eric faced/ is facing the losses and changes in his life—his will to metamorphose—awed his medical team, his family, his strong circle of friends. The invalid who refuses to be in-valid. Diane Raptosh "erics America" both because "America is the nation-expression of/a severely traumatized person" and, it seems to me, because she has challenged herself, and her readers, to encounter what she knows of America (and Western Civilization more deeply), from capitalism to global warming to COVID to Trump and beyond—"a place where the horror's normal"—with the resolve and openness to reinvention her brother's example has provided. "Can you love in a country that slaughters its children" the book asks. The poems that result are mythic (re-mythic), bodily, seeking, agile, generous and capacious, and for all that the poet vows to "crowdsource/ a term that kneecaps certitude," ultimately hopeful in their will to go on.

—Christine Gelineau, *Appetite for the Divine*

Nearly two hundred years after Whitman heard America singing, Diane Raptosh hears it clanging— and her instinct, rather than to mourn the cacophony, is to pick apart the notes that create it. Despite one of the more memorable lines here, these are not poems of "fateful steps in a clear-cut direction." Raptosh's approach is to assault the foundations of language as well as those of her country, twisting *America* into a near-rhyme and wondering if the nation will reduce the lack of her to a catchphrase. Through fragments of Leonard Bernstein, precarious family members and the apathetic loom of corporations, these poems form a sketch of an author who views her art as incitement—maybe the key to a new origin story, even if it requires "rewrit[ing] the pen" to tell it.

—Michael Miller, *Tea and Subtitles*

I
Eric
America
POEMS

Diane Raptosh

Etruscan Press

Etruscan Press
Wilkes University
84 West South Street
Wilkes-Barre, PA 18766
(570) 408-4546

Wilkes University

www.etruscanpress.org

Published 2024 by Etruscan Press
Printed in the United States of America
Cover art: *a person standing in the air with a star in their hand*, The Metaverse, 2021
© Julien Tromeur
Cover design by Lisa Reynolds
Interior design and typesetting by Kari Bayait
The text of this book is set in Iowan.

First Edition

17 18 19 20 5 4 3 2 1

Library of Congress Cataloguing-in-Publication Data

Names: Raptosh, Diane, author. Title: I Eric America / Diane Raptosh.
Description: First edition. | Wilkes-Barre, PA : Etruscan Press, 2024. |
Summary: "Raptosh's collection of sonnets combines elements of family trauma (her brother Eric's survival of a plane crash and subsequent paraplegia) with disturbances on the national stage. Equal parts origin story, myth, and song, the book unfolds from the premise that America is the nation-expression of / a severely traumatized person"-- Provided by publisher.
Identifiers: LCCN 2024011104 | ISBN 9798988198550 (trade paperback)
Subjects: LCGFT: Poetry.
Classification: LCC PS3568.A634 I15 2024 | DDC 811/.54--dc23/eng/20240506
LC record available at https://lccn.loc.gov/2024011104
Please turn to the back of this book for a list of the sustaining funders of Etruscan Press.

America is a person.

—Joy Harjo

Contents

I

A key, a cell phone, a piece of paper and a pen. And one of my gray hairs, whose atoms preserve the memory of the origins of life, of the cosmic Catastrophe that gave the world its beginning.

—Olga Tokarczuk

In this origin story, the moon crowns three people:
the mother, her children. In the original vision,
a girl might birth her own brother. In this roiling
storehouse: relics from Delos, Sicily. Safe vests
for travel to Mars. In origin-storage: bloodroot.
Wet bulb. Torsi. Here and there, worry seeps in
to rewrite the corm of the fathers. In its oaring
through woe, the tale will take in some deer. A dog.
This story's original flora count locusts. Dogwood.
Fir trees. This tale refers to the genus of shrub
artemisia, holy mother of absinthe. Don't you just
love how *absinthe* abs its way right smack into the
in the—exactly how epics start out: *In the beginning,*
maybe a girl ago, an original glory brined everyone kin—

To sing in the presence of quaking
is to summon the cosmic being. I have
been trying to walk a theistic path
with tactical feet like a row of ghost deer.
I am just beginning to grok that the bunch
of white male slave owners, then in
their twenties, were pretty much lame-ass
system designers. So, if you're sensing
an edginess, lady, the lap of the world
is a map of the unmet needs of men's pain.
And *money*—the miscreant word for *I need*
some warmth to protect me. My old honey
locust to rock me. A smooth lunular amulet.
That place within us which isn't yet gouged.

My brother Eric and I are not twins

but trauma bonds hinge and entwine us

why at age twelve and nine we hoisted

our mother to life from her bed-mitten

five decades later Eric flew he fluttered

he fell from a sky that cleavered his spine

his femur his head left his neck so lightly

he dervished whole noted the day the plane

lofted then failed dubbed that second an age

the day Eric slapped through the air I yanked

my scream into birth-giving leaned in to stroke

his chair rims dice the dried prunes dole out cleft

Gabapentin god I throat them myself out of hope

of finding a sleeping position his pain maybe isn't

For my summer body, I would like

two pairs of buttocks: that populous

softness. An owl face peeping from my navel—

my gown-surround, a flock of orange

feathers. I'd want to have gold-red hair

and grebes' lobed feet. I'd like even

the clefts of my knees to wreak *bosom*.

I want to pay egrets rent as I rise

from a basket of corn ears. I'd like to

serve up a torso of locust and fir tree,

angle and star husk—six hundred eaves'

daydreams of tones sieved from the tissues

of language. I want every aged ripeness

to die in my care. I want everyone born here.

The New Moon in Aquarius Wants You
to Work for Change, says *Astrology.com.*
I therefore un-don the order of tiepin,
declare the deer human and ode around
the room on doe-eared tiptoe. I am told
that the moon will trine with the Node
of Fate in the North. It may just sound odd,
but the Greek root of beauty is *calling.*
I might not have to marry a bed, throw up
my hands. It's clear how the goose egg's
lack of *care for* keeps laying its background.
The aqueous moon wants everyone's *we*
to wage queer dissent: to baseline a doe
to quarry past light to free-range an eon.

If the *I* is an inn, how do I *you*

from inside my pee-yewy nosebag,

my wired maw bra, this cotton serape

of separateness? Today in my mask:

a trail of foundation. A lone eyelash. One

lipstick schmear: *Huntress*. A snick of

bear smell. Dear *you:* In this microbial

cloud dithers the sonnet, its nets of notes

sent to tens of no ones. Its tectonic runes.

Its honed stone mansions, its zoos of

hosannas. So, too—*say it!*—my own

Roman nose hews its tendons of snot

toward the plains' rock song—that plum

neon ode: the sun-luxed onset of oneness.

The previous president's mixing of symbols
and language of his campaign with the language
and symbols of state was surely illegal. So, too,
his unprocessed pain: vaccinated into everyone's
vein. Which could be the global virus Covid blew in
to reframe. The state can't look after itself, and frankly,

it blows how no one makes a federal case out of that.
The Plague of Justinian erased almost a third of mankind—
plus rewrote the fates of a couple of empires. I've spent
the better half of my days gnawing America's toothpick.
Raked its mouthfeel. Ladled my tongue round its layers
of con. Its trove of *me*-cameras. Its rows of crown merch.
I'm shocked this isn't illegal: how assonance mic's its mini-
subversions. How saying *crepuscular* helps you spot a deer.

is there a name for one who walks like a deer

is there a term for the sounds of keyboard typing

are there words for the *step-step | pause | step-step* cadence

any better year to root out untongued pain

any verb for how bucks jut their front legs out from the body

is the deer-foot a lesson in form and function

does the doe offer classes in fusing the senses

can the doe hear a heart pound from fifteen yards

why do deer carve hoofprints in upside-down hearts

how to count *step-step | pause | step-step* cadence

is there one word for *cells to a body ≥ souls to a nation*

how to scan deer leaping down an embankment

what's the noun for *she who rouses is also a voice of caution*

is there a foot named for fateful steps in a clear-cut direction

I like to sit so still I burst my known

borders, blur into torso, slide into

unity. I wait to let formlessness slake

and forgive me: It sees I'm so *there*

that I'm not, it sieves me to layers of

cinders and lime and then dubs me a shine

of the moon—both dirge and a birthstone,

the mind inside everyone. To put it

cleanly, I come undone. And doing so,

hope to reline the bounds of my name—

to christen *to Di* as shorthand for *birth*

new ways to emerge, tag the me you,

decide no I *is mine*. With this, to sift new

bloodroots. To dodge ruin doing so.

In an essay called "The Last Diana"
is pictured the Head of Christ: a detail
of Figure 10, *The Sarcophagus of
Christ Giving the Law,* from the Musée
de l'Arles et de la Provence antiques.
The pate of Christ looks to the author's eye
like the heads of ancient Dianas. And it's true
of Christ's profile: that privately opened
mouth, the ripe upper lids. That small
transition of skin between forehead and
furrow carved near his chancel of hair.
Even Christ's curls mimic her roving
tresses—their axes of scrolls this maze of
helix, this heaven sheveled in question marks.

I want to found a new pronoun that bridges

the gap between self and bromeliad,

lichen and fire ant, bedlam and boredom.

I'm going to breed a new pronoun poised

to make power wake afraid—to endstop

its fits and free throws. Undo its home brews.

Each *now*, I plan to see each *thou* as they

are and not as cut-outs from earlier trauma.

I plan to nutmeg this vowel-meringue noun

with equal jots boundlessness and dissolution,

lay it in leaf-litter berms. I vow to crowdsource

a term that kneecaps certitude. That donkeys

around in a global cleanse of identity—every cell

bowed and braying *Xah* to new blue nonets of suns.

All the good words have become corporations:

Marmot. Prismatic. Sublime Electric. Still,

the song woodchucks on—through its caches

of berries. Its ratio of grasses, its stints

with bent light. The song knows to roll

to the mood of its voltas. To missile its lines

through the twinned boardrooms of *Sonnet*

Technologies. The song woodchucks wood,

mulches live rock—the woodchuck of psalm

whistling on like it is Mutiny's very prairie dog.

How fast the croon slivers up! Just how much

wood must one chew off America's nattering

toothpick? Besides. How much good does it do

to the marmot busy subliming its prisms?

Might the virus stretch out an apocalypse evenly
Might the line break release a life-based economy
Have you tried using *Xah* as your personal pronoun
Can you love in a country that slaughters its children
Do poems give me what some get from mothers
Does the word *Xana* spring from the Latin *Diana*
Should we just *Ave Maria* the mishap America
Might the volta give rise to joy-based economies
Ever sensed you're the *esse* of doe in a filter of person
In these shafts of attention is some sentience present
At that question's behest, can you queer the unseen
Can't you see I'm bastilled by this sonnet's free rein
How I bust out *Marias* to caretake a nation
Ever met my Labrador pup, Leonard Bernstein

Okay. I'm going to start today over

tomorrow, end its to-dos with these

toy dots: *Ta-da.* For starters, I'm going

to end my tryst with the Tao. I'm done

not voicing its mutes—the Ways of Heaven

shuck and confuse. The tsunami of nations

spares no bloom due to fragrance. I spurn

inexertion. So, I suddenly feel I must ask

you to pause as I mate with the "f" sound—

    ^   ^ ^   ^ ^   <****>^ ^ . . . . Hereafter,

I plan to *enverb* proper nouns, to *Đạo Mẫu*

the *wu* and its *wei*. I accordion flutes,

I un-white the true. I wholly re-estrus

a world that rivers its hips in fits of un-fear.

Defying most ancient of rifts
between worlds outside and in,   ,
I find I've been living a double
life: the timed and the mythic.
Gills and hind legs. Dry land,
the etheric. This dares to stow
hope in my throat sac—the fact
the whole day's been secreting
its twin, nighttime. Its surrogate
sheen helps me to slip into second-
person perspective, grind the lens
of my *I* into you, subject each
verb to the *unto* and quietly
skin-breathe this quarto of sonnets.

When I become dust, I want *to Diane*
to be human for *Do not repeat where*
we were. I want it to shorthand how-to's.
How to upend: First, we re-nature. I want it
to plug for the land while sizing up griefs
of the day. To show how to stand for the self
while penciling notes on the trim of the world:
Why it's queer to feel cared for: It's a fact about
life in America. I would like my own action
verb to bank and clearwing. I want *to id*
and lever a din that heaps insistence on *us*
in the spore of its origin story. To have sung
as a sample person sheltering Earth. For you
to have oared these lines by the strobe of Venus.

II

*Everything you love will probably be lost, but in the end,
love will return in another way.*

—Franz Kafka

With umpteen fourteeners I can spin lines from truth's future.

Turns out my single mom angst worked great as seeing-eye dog.

Each day the rheumy red tie turned on to air out its id.

So, while stroking our pets, we could still score dopamine hits.

A cat's pheromone-sense is fourteen times keener than humans'.

Fourteeners are whiskers tuned to the in-house canticle.

The U.S.: mendacity's chainsaw art airbrushed in prayer.

Fourteeners are mountain feet—fourteen thousand or more.

We need a new slant to arrive at an ore of pure truth.

So, I'll warble on about whiteness's ravenousness:

something so *there* it swore it was not, like melees of snow

in an avalanche. It couched itself in *so whats*—until

it spied in the white of its own wack eye both whip and veil.

So, *phew*. Also, to sum up: So what if I eat myself.

Is it true for you too: The greasier your hair,

the bolder the feeling? *En garde*: I live somewhat

in fear of the stare of the colon, but its steadiness

serves its own form of protest—honor—this song

is an earful. Sincerely: I'm afraid to feel cared for.

I fear that Big Pharma will end up our principal

ancestor. I worry my region's so red that Covid

might jigger our county back to stage three.

I'd say it's quite the appropriate sentence: Just

look at us—locking up sheep and cuffing our egg-

laying hens. Traveling cows await incumbency

in concentration camps. Their blowy brown eyes

endear and serene me. They dare me to log this

remonstrance: to rewrite the pen: to deputize mercy.

Within America's innards is
a car cam are aerials of Mars is
a line of cream for your ire is
a demesne of Mace cans is
the em dash's ram ears is
where Eric's rope arms are
the hunt and the chase-ism
where absinthe of caste sips
where rats are where rice is
where arms mic the state is
where absence's tribes live
what ICE is to racism:
Inside this place is the make of
a person in fear of his basement

I've always feared the loneliness of marriage.
So I've looked for something else to forge
new bond songs from. My latest someone
does not fill me with love's robberies.
Because he took me up with the tongue.
Because when he talks to himself he knows
to call his I *we*. May I add how it matters
he lapped me like a Reuben sandwich.
Because: *marbled rye*. Because: *corned*.
Because: *buttered sides out*. Because hot
begets warm. Because that *hūs* within *husband*
means home. Because *būa,* to dwell. Because
face it: that triple-decker of exes. Because
hope bonds those whose heat needs two houses.

Diandry is the practice of having two
husbands. So, when the loan officer
at my bank slips me the royal we as she
asks, *Are we single or married?* I can say
yes. What we mean is I'm bride to that
species of monarch whose hues let it honor
the Prince of Orange. Out of time, I married
the state. Eric's wheelchair rims. A neighboring
Cooper's hawk. Have we signaled I'm marred—
avoidant attachment style? I'm sorry this segue
is so weird. I'm oafish. I'm armed. I cannot
take love. Why else sit here for months days years
in the corm and dung of an unhurried lingua,
bloom and botch of the *we* owling for vowels?

To steady my mother, I wedded her.

Rebirthed, ribboned and pillared her.

To steady her meant I would probably

replicate: chugalug rat poison. Marry

a bitch-ass dude, mother Mr. America.

To have stirred my own mom to survival

made me both parent and my own child,

an addict to rein and rescue. So, I have to

just ask: How in the torn wick of time

can the nation improve if my ear is not

slicked to its ground 24/7? Ah let me go

mic Eric's chair: Watch how I chum others'

pain without tracing my own, the words now

starting to grieve too much & this one has a cough—

I want to name America my brother,

since we all see that *eric* stashed in

the navel of nation-state. I want the union

to man an inner change of location, to shift

from the seed of *Eric* meaning *one, alone,*

unique, to its roots in *long-time journey,*

everlasting, eternity. I would like the place

to navel-gaze just enough to note that

dogwood's frail stateliness. To annotate

decency. To nightly simulcast grace. I'd like

the state to glide on its rims, scuffed and

abraded, forging new rubrics of spine. I'd like

the nation to state out loud: *All that rage—at last*

—is what pain feels like when I air it in public.

Time keeps trying to turn over—torn
core like Eric's in his weeks in ICU.
The red sign at the edge of his bed:
Log Roll Only. That's how you transfer
the body of trauma. It's how things swerve
as timelessness grazes the time-bound gorge.
That's how scenes trend when the age
is a patient: half grit, half paralysis. This,
how truth chuffs from its long spine board—
lewd power rivered to all the wrong places.
That red sign showed a raft of stick figures
ready to logroll a patient: one with twig hands
along heart-vine and hip, one reigning over
the head—all others, both-sidesing the invalid.

Eric is a typically masculine name

Eric means *versatile benevolent brave*

Eric is made of the element *ei—always ever eternal*

Eric means *very prince of the air*

Eric means *ever restless in change*

A *rikr* means *ruler,* let's say Erik the Red

Erik the Red: first permanent European settler

One form of Eric means *way too cozy with force*

Eric is sometimes taken to mean *autocrat*

Eric is a superfund site of creaturely pain

Eric can expand in any direction according to will

Ask how many tenses man his inner nation

I hear America clanging, the various Erics there are

America means *the eternal state of what never quite came*

Chimerical is my favorite near rhyme

for *America*: fire breather + serpent's

prayer: ~20% rich ÷ 80% poor. A fightin'

judge in a chair | the craw of a George C.

Wallace + torso of John Wilkes Booth.

Infinitive split at the root. Purple carrot

complete with a tiny white buttock inside.

The sadness of Jesus's breasts × the fuss

of the Artemis Space Program. Alchemical

math on meth. Heart sutra licked into smut.

That summitless mountaintop intermixed w/

a ghostly stag grinding its hooves = enough

weed that the pain is there and I am gone. So

too the mythos of *all:* that knot. Its sweat trickle.

The song must be cultural confessional
Sicilian-school peasant tune aria prayer
Roman law Troubador *fin'amor* mothers
carpenters logic inwardness argument chaos
impulse estrus safehouse cicadas typhoons
fire-belt megaflood drought-belt diasporas'
buckle rub reader the song must never not
have at dark money's white lightning lobbed
atop poor rich worlds where billionauts preen
here weaning their thug henchmen their tizzy
of flagellants gives me to say the song wants
mostly to thank you to fetch you no shoo-in
verb as it scans the view deciding to plink a plain
little tunk-a-tunk when finally the tanks arrive

I step out in the world and always feel torn.

It feels like even the ending's burning.

California oranges every sky across Idaho.

Seems now even the sun screams porno.

I live in a place where the horror's normal.

System just hocks up ways to uniamb me.

It's a racket, everyone's personhood stolen.

Nation says it'll make great use of unDiane.

Everyone hews a name that cannot be spoken.

Nation says *Show me the worth of your being*

simply by naming someone weaker inhuman.

Song sets its tune to the dying in everyone.

Country spells *rot* and *torn* and *cur* and *crony,*

fire howling its tithes to the giver of language.

My dad went AWOL when I was a child.
So, the realm of the fathers no longer
slips me their mickeys. Still, I feel heaviness
wheeze from this threefold split: loonies
who fight, leaders who flee, and the state
that's so numbed it seems spinally orphaned.
Real action is not reaction but a creation.
The West's biggest threat is the world it made.
Who birthed the oligarchs? We did. Listen.
I fixate. Repair. I way overcompensate,
egg on and over-care. It's as if once I leave
my house, I'm having sex or at war with
everything out there. Every second is like that.
Each beat, I squirm around in the gutter of it.

Everything is a plane crash every jet wheel

flung from the char's far deck its hulls and

arcs this crash cart volt shock this fuselage shin

its rattletrap lash our family warping its fangs

aileron mourning its wings Eric the use of his legs

each night we blame we ravel the sky a laid up

democracy slinging each grain to the top that

cough that scrofula liftoff uprush look America

chortled its joy through a plane's chained air it

barked that day it roared its mask off O Eric's legs

fly apart when they come unbelted oxygen blazes

its hospital bed this empennage ash every bit part

claims its scritch and yaw as snowflecks capsize

most of April Autofill scrawls the month *Paris*

America is the nation-expression of
a severely traumatized person. Which
makes me a human hair-trigger. I really am
made of my brother, caught between
Jedi torso and nerve-wracked numbness
boothed in the lower half of the body. Yes,
we're merely a swarm to thin before Musk
and Bezos jet their glitz-pilgrims to Mars—
the Artemis lunar landing, host of a layover
hitched to the red trajectory. I fear these pretty
much tetchy jottings will really tick off my hair.
Psst, Eric: Let us un-die. Let us din and naiad
ideas that flipper in Earth-joy. Ooh let me retire
from nation re-rigging until the ends of my name.

Why didn't the Vikings colonize America

Is Eric a nation within a nation

Is the U.S. a mannequin of unfelt grief

Are America's pronouns *I my mine*

Is Eric secretly cheeking his meds

Is America a race of re-namers

Is America clans of deer atop mountains of vowels

Is America about to make an announcement

Is Eric basically everyone's kin

Is America's main entrée meanness

Is America's epithet *crime syndicate*

Is America brought to you by the look of Christ

Is Eric's narrative parable

Is Christ's face principally female

III

These scars bear witness but whether to repair or to destruction
I no longer know.

–Adrienne Rich

If you're looking for a miracle, / look to the invisible.

–Alice Fulton

After the plane crash Eric had to ab
his way back into *entity*—yeti on fins
kinetic bitcoin on sprigs on pinions in
process on tektitic teeth on batty pain
meds on acid an ocelot mostly half eaten
of human canoe of rims of a fledgling
phage an aged penny smell so exquisite
his abscessed cheek some gold-eyed opah
razzing his acres of hair its haywire net
its scalp-mite shores its toothsome babies
its chest hair's silverfish grit in fists on
ricks of forgiving this blow as Christ's
own teats as one-fourth tree in wet bulb
temps his one compound eye crossed

Maybe you've seen the YouTube: Leonard Bernstein
conducting Haydn's Symphony 88, 4th Movement
with only his face—ear-flare replacing left wrist-
flick, eyebrow adjusts the rubato. That chin-drop:
a man with forty faces per minute. Reminds me
how memory knows to groom its own genre.
How fast the *rubato* drums out from *rob*. At 0:09
his top lip rekeys a rote mother-sorrow. This adds
to subtraction from last-place catastrophe. We all
know to conduct is not to reveal what the score is
anyhow. The smirk says he knows the strings play
the note on tempo in sync. You can't hear the grin
but can feel how the end knows to square with it:
heat domes. Ash face of the hegemon. The body of
Leonard, this whirl-stilled village staking its heavens.

When Eric and I lifted our mom from her bed-

mitten we both of us yes we tilt into Mars

we rear we earful we rue we wolfpaw

on slurry we altar we fetal her pin-bones

& fleet we float we *di* we two unruin her

bruise we *eric* we beetle we roam atop

urine we mama the mom we earful us raw

we tom-tom we pretty we reroof a womb

we facecloth we yucca rookiest blossoms

we trot we currycomb O we curlicue mons

gnaw rag rugs we werewolf we ovum us

shower her *tsk* we worry the AWOL father

we sepal we man the whole state of her sop up

we rooftop *Whee* we done rerun her innards

My mom, Lenny Bernstein and I share a birthday:

August 25th. I keep going back to that

YouTube so I can read time on Len's face:

incarnadine oils—their rucked patois, their

mom particles. *Just think of those unflat*

ways in which thought unfolds—the choice

between line and sphere, inks Lenny's grin—

right ear mining eternities, left ear ovaling

question marks: *Who gets to live? How, shape*

sounds through a human face? And finally,

who will get what? And that according to riches?

Race? Demagogue? To become denatured is

to be indentured. Now if you'll excuse me here

for a sec: I think I hear a mama cry up in line six.

Between you and me, I want to just sit here
and riverine. Which helps me steady-eye
fear number one: that I was put here to
feel into song what runnels the human,
but I'm unfit to be one. Someone might
call this *being aligned with your purpose.*
That just smears the embarrassment.
Today some spine of wheat in me keeled.
Teeth in their blotchy fur sweaters. I figure
the senses exist to tell us it's time to retreat
from the earth once they hardly work. Hm.
Has this always been here. Silt in my eye.
I can't smell anymore. Here, a beached onion.
I have no one to world this to but poetry.

Every tree, every beast, every place is
a person-faced thing to whom I would like
to say *Step in my studio|station, please just
let me re-myth you, rowing through music.*
The first word I ever learned to spell was *office*.
The second, *dependable.* That child is an age
in myself, the way cities and towns are human
places—the nation, simply idea. My brother
and I share a butte-shaped interior. The city lost
out to the nation-state. As I have tried to steady
America, ends keep surging. Because its name
is a euphony. Because alms birth plosives. Ah,
muy rica, yes, its open-end ruckus. Because
this place feels so loveless, I think I'll go veg.

I'd like to trill you a song about end-words.

Moon about how many tenses there could be.

Mountain Time knolls to the mouth of eternity.

Nighttime knows to sling its lune in broad light.

Today I'll sweep five sun rinds into my nightie.

Napping all day noons into *mad reclamation of self*.

Anyhow, *Moon's* now short for *Onward to Mars*.

On board will be seated a pair of phantom torsos—

Helga + Zohar to deck in the lower spacecraft.

Only the latter to wear that cool protective vest.

The word Zohar vines from *those who are wise*.

I hereby dub Mme. Zohar my *muse-statuette*.

I'd like to family-farm a new tense—thing is,

Zohar's stoic torso keeps thumping on about zeds.

Zohar, in biblical terms your core, your name's
root vaunts the brightness of heavens. Listen.
I saved all the rubrics to pixel and muse you,
Ghost Sim and sister—38 slices of mimed
human tissue, my fetish mimosa: my whipsaw
stage of latest reflection. My Clio, my Fanny,
my phantom Diana, my Beatrice. My favored
Rx for restlessness. Mme. Neal Cassady, mini
Polymnia. One squint at Blake's Zoas harpoons
how it makes me feel nervy and freer when, singing,
I think of you, thank the whole stump of whom
I will view as long as dawns leaven: I vow to
just couch here to fledge and ensoul you, to suds
and to ode you, from euphony's Canaan of liftoff—

Bezos Smooths a Path toward Lunar Deliveries.

Are Plans Being Made to Brew Beer on the Moon?

Deep Space Entices Upstarts and Mainstays.

You Cannot Reach the Moon in Your Mercedes.

Bibles Flown to Moon Stir Ownership Dispute.

Entrance to Underground Cave Found on the Moon.

New Film Shows How NASA 'Faked Apollo Mission.'

Backyard Bass Take Bait Behind the Moon.

Massive Asteroid to Safely Cruise Past Earth.

How Can We Tell When Objects Clip the Moon?

Holy Temple Planned for the Moon's South Pole.

You: Part Owner of the Moon and Stars by Law. No Joke.

America's Plan to Nuke the Moon: Another Cold War Plot.

We Know the Pink Moon's Coming, But What's That?

Seems the whole world is becoming America.

Fruit cooks on trees, shellfish lace shorelines.

Covid and Earth-warming: centers of profit.

You may see me as cuffed to the sonnet—a bit

like how money gets lashed to the hands of the few.

I'm told when my needs aren't met, I use critique

as stand-in for closeness. Today's horoscope lists

these to-dos: scalpel, tweezers, pick axe. *Don'ts:*

flinch, stunt-double, get locked in the *ugh*-interior.

It suggests that to level the score, I apologize. For

shifting to nation those pains I have shunned: pluck

my heart|lung|liver. Flit these to the air in an antique

vessel. Yes. Can. Will. Just after I Bernstein the ache

of the people, launching batons from the ship of my face—

I confess I am part of the error America

My pink heart carries a Glock Nineteen

My inner con man wants to fool Eric

I store spite vibes in my sciatic nerve

I offer critique when I need to feel cherished

If I feel defeated I say that the country is

I threw a red brick through my neighbor's window

I left a tray of dove seed out for the deer

I like this place I like the idea of this place

I would like the palace of ideas to have more sway

I swear then I long to say something beautiful

If I use the *I* too much I start to feel shame

When Eric has a bad pain day he names it Diane

When I feel like dissing a thing I call it America

As the age grows more paralyzed, my asthma

gets worse. The ducks of my lungs wade around

in what feels like barley malt syrup. The nude

violinist shanked in my ribs mothers four strings,

which bloodroots a quaver of notes. To begin

to chorale new patterns is to practice reversals:

I promise my heart I won't blunt its rhythms simply

by living. I won't brace the feet of the air. It may

be all right to let something feel easy. I'll keep

verbing nouns to re-border people and places—

to form a new *now* when time comes unnumbed.

For today, let me Mars the earth's nerve-pain. Let

the mauled world not mimic America. Re: the giver

of language—go ahead, viol the moon's gonzo orbit.

Sixteenets with Notes App

[B]ind to labours / of day & night the myriads of Eternity.

—William Blake

The inner witness, my finest defect:

4/1/22 My outer fitness finesses this

Verdict: a nation so crippled

4/2/22 it can't even punish a coup

It started with selling off public goods

Yesterday to private ownership

That loan officer asked my *us*

6/5/21 Have we ever declared bankruptcy?

In the attention economy

6/8/21 every action is a transaction. Test:

Lose everything from the waist down

9/5/20 $3,542.79 in Eric's GoFundMe

Rims. Bibs. List: What you will not let stand

6/6/21 in the We. *Have we ever inquired*

What dark money steals as I write

1:29 PM They call it dark but it's white

Watch how deer twitch into their bodies

6/30/21   Here, the non-where eyes you

Listen to *Cellphone's Dead* by Beck

6/13/21   It's about how it's about it

Set up a new Voicemail Password

5/10/21   00diane00 no caps

True this: I straddle two time zones

Thursday and its eternities

The first time I turned 60 I was age 9

Yesterday *Kinked daisy hatched in cactus*

This time I busily strip my *I*

3:44 PM   for its qualia, use those as quarry

I feel so I figure I know how to *eric*

4:00 PM   If I had freed myself wholly

from the wound could I have reversed

4:01 PM the way the earth has gone

Whiten for Life, vows the sign at the dentist

6/29/21 More or less sums up America

Midsummer's read: *Outcome of Covid on White*

7/9/21 *-Collar Crime:* Won't find it in FBI data

If they can disappear a thing in language

Yesterday No additional text

New Social Security ID: 8XZXXXYX

4:32 PM $14.24 in Eric's GoFundMe

Torn world-core halts to reiterate

4:33 PM time's running over: Logs roll

unwailed pain into everyone:

4:59 PM Crude strain of a leave-in conditioner

This flesh is a mystery airbrushed to center-

6:00 PM fold summer which grumbles *inferno*

Love is a luge, a pulse, a day-glo phage

Yesterday Pick up Eric a dry-board calendar

It's a decolonization project: Say it

9:45 PM as if *as is* means *with*

People mean things & so don't say them

Yesterday right yeah huh yeah right wait

What arrows fly true will group tightly

Yesterday —isn't what I'd call black magic

How to word my way around this state

1/1/22 Feel pain? *Go blacken someone*

Mussolini, pure clown | Hitler was lazy

1/6/22 anniversary of the dress rehearsal

A too-muchness often turns ruinous

1/7/22 Autocracy Inc.: *Moola's Ironmen*

No oil on Mars LOL, that we know of—

1/8/22 nickel|iron|chlorine|sulfur|titanium

Deep space will never hear the people

12:00 AM hold the *each* in the toothache tree

The polity's paralyzed

11:59 AM Americans are split

Henceforward one side must take over

Yesterday That means: head, the father

American power—in property

Yesterday simply protects slave owners

Let's start with the question

12:00 PM of being deserving. Being deserted

The Office of Internal Cruelty: blaming

1:00 PM others for free-range fragility

Who or what is an actual person—

1:15 PM It. Who gets to survive

Am trying to stay hitched to the world

Yesterday brushing my dog Lenny Bernstein

Well, if you don't like it here

Yesterday you can just move to eternity—

Acknowledgements

The author wishes to thank the following journals and anthologies in which many of these poems, sometimes in different versions, originally appeared: *Limberlost Review; Northwest Review; ROOM: A Sketchbook for Analytic Action 2.23* and *6.23; The Cabin: MOON: Writers in the Attic; The Cabin: RUPTURE: Writers in the Attic; The Night's Magician: Poems about the Moon; The Polaris Trilogy: Poems for the Moon; The Trick is to Keep Breathing: COVID 19 Stories from African and North American Writers, Vol. 3; The Power of the Feminine I.*

With profound gratitude for kindness and support from

Nin Andrews, C.R. Austin, Phil Brady, Gina Centioli, Keats Raptosh Conley, Dallas Gudgell, Diane Jarvenpa, Robin Lorentzen, Alan Minskoff, Robert Mooney, Joe Morgan, Debbra Palmer, Amanda Rabaduex, Colette Raptosh, Camas Schaeffer, Weston Schaeffer, Melanie Schroeder, Karley Stasko, Rodrigo Toscano, Pamela Turchin, and all the fine people at Etruscan Press.

*Note on the Sixteenets: These "sixteenets" are collaborations between the poet and the iPhone's NotesApp, including its time stamps and koan-like, fragmented couplet effects.

Bezos Smooths a Path toward Lunar Deliveries was composed entirely of headlines culled from various news sources.

About the Author

Diane Raptosh's fourth book of poetry, *American Amnesiac* (Etruscan Press), was longlisted for the 2013 National Book Award and was a finalist for the Housatonic Book Award. The recipient of three fellowships in literature from the Idaho Commission on the Arts, she served as the Boise Poet Laureate (2013) as well as the Idaho Writer-in-Residence (2013-2016). In 2018, she won the Idaho Governor's Arts Award in Excellence. A highly active ambassador for poetry, she has given poetry workshops everywhere from riverbanks to maximum security prisons. She teaches literature and creative writing and co-directs the program in Criminal Justice/Prison Studies at the College of Idaho.

Books from Etruscan Press

Zarathustra Must Die | Dorian Alexander
The Disappearance of Seth | Kazim Ali
The Last Orgasm | Nin Andrews
Drift Ice | Jennifer Atkinson
Crow Man | Tom Bailey
Coronology | Claire Bateman
Viscera | Felice Belle
Reading the Signs and other itinerant essays | Stephen Benz
Topographies | Stephen Benz
What We Ask of Flesh | Remica L. Bingham
The Greatest Jewish-American Lover in Hungarian History | Michael Blumenthal
No Hurry | Michael Blumenthal
Choir of the Wells | Bruce Bond
Cinder | Bruce Bond
The Other Sky | Bruce Bond and Aron Wiesenfeld
Peal | Bruce Bond
Scar | Bruce Bond
Until We Talk | Darrell Bourque and Bill Gingles
Poems and Their Making: A Conversation | Moderated by Philip Brady
Crave: Sojourn of a Hungry Soul | Laurie Jean Cannady
Toucans in the Arctic | Scott Coffel
Sixteen | Auguste Corteau
Don't Mind Me | Brian Coughlan
Wattle & daub | Brian Coughlan
Body of a Dancer | Renée E. D'Aoust
Generations: Lullaby with Incendiary Device, The Nazi Patrol, and How It Is That We | Dante Di Stefano, William Heyen, and H. L. Hix
Ill Angels | Dante Di Stefano
Aard-vark to Axolotl: Pictures From my Grandfather's Dictionary | Karen Donovan
Trio: Planet Parable, Run: A Verse-History of Victoria Woodhull, and Endless Body | Karen Donovan, Diane Raptosh, and Daneen Wardrop
Scything Grace | Sean Thomas Dougherty
Areas of Fog | Will Dowd
Romer | Robert Eastwood
Wait for God to Notice | Sari Fordham
Bon Courage: Essays on Inheritance, Citizenship, and a Creative Life | Ru Freeman
Surrendering Oz | Bonnie Friedman
Funeral Playlist | Sarah Gorham
Nahoonkara | Peter Grandbois
Triptych: The Three-Legged World, In Time, and Orpheus & Echo | Peter Grandbois, James McCorkle, and Robert Miltner
The Candle: Poems of Our 20th Century Holocausts | William Heyen
The Confessions of Doc Williams & Other Poems | William Heyen
The Football Corporations | William Heyen
A Poetics of Hiroshima | William Heyen
September 11, 2001: American Writers Respond | Edited by William Heyen
Shoah Train | William Heyen
American Anger: An Evidentiary | H. L. Hix

Etruscan Press Is Proud of Support Received From

Wilkes University

Ohio Arts Council

The Stephen & Jeryl Oristaglio Foundation

Community of Literary Magazines and Presses

National Endowment for the Arts

Drs. Barbara Brothers & Gratia Murphy Endowment

Founded in 2001 with a generous grant from the Oristaglio
Foundation, Etruscan Press is a nonprofit cooperative of poets
and writers working to produce and promote books that nurture
the dialogue among genres, achieve a distinctive voice, and
reshape the literary and cultural histories of which we are a part.

Etruscan Press
www.etruscanpress.org
Etruscan Press books may be ordered from

Consortium Book Sales and Distribution
800.283.3572
www.cbsd.com

Etruscan Press is a 501(c)(3) nonprofit organization.
Contributions to Etruscan Press are tax deductible
as allowed under applicable law.
For more information, a prospectus,
or to order one of our titles,
contact us at books@etruscanpress.org.

Printed in the USA
CPSIA information can be obtained
at www.ICGtesting.com
JSHW021255110924
69690JS00001B/3